EVERYTHING YOU NEED TO KNOW
ABOUT VENDING MACHINE BUSINESS:
Costs, Tips, Pros & Cons

Britta J Parker

INTRODUCTION

If you've ever enjoyed your time choosing a snack from a decent selection in of you, a peek into the vending machine might be for you. In addition to chips and lemonades, vending machines now offer healthy snacks and even electronic or pharmacy items. It can be a very lucrative side business or a full-time operation. Here's what you need to know to get started.

Vending machines are by no means a new business idea - after all, they can be found everywhere. But for those of you looking to start your own business, there's a lot to like about the vending industry. Consider that there are millions of machines in the US alone - and the vending machine industry is worth over $23 billion in annual sales. Reason enough to start your own vending machine business.

Table of Contents

Chapter 1

How to start a vending machine business: a step-by-step guide.

Chapter 2

Pros and cons of starting a vending machine business.

Advantages and disadvantages

Chapter 3

frequently asked Questions.

Chapter 4

Advantages of a vending machine shop.

Chapter 1

How to start a vending machine business: a step-by-step guide

Any advantage or insight you have about vending machines is a great way to break into this niche business. For example, if you've already identified a need for a vending machine in your area, reach out to property owners you know and gauge their interest in installing vending machines at their locations.

But even without personal connections, you can open a vending machine business – and earn money with it. How to start a vending machine business in six steps.

1. Consider your vending machine options

While most people think that vending machines only come in the standard snack and soda varieties, if you've thought about how to start a vending machine business you probably know that there are more options. In general, there are four different categories of vending machines (which we will outline below). Consider all four types when choosing the machine whose products resonate best with your target market.

Whatever type of machine you choose, start with one or two machines with a specific market focus. This allows you to gradually learn popular inventory and site-specific patterns and add new machines accordingly.

Sale of food and drinks

According to Vending Market Watch's 2019 annual report, food and beverage vending machines that sell snack foods, sodas, and candy account for the bulk of the vending market share in the U.S., with beverages alone accounting for nearly a third of vending sales. If you're wondering how to start a vending machine business, you can't go wrong with this old standard.

Of course, there are variations on this standard - you can get a machine that only offers drinks, snacks, or snack-and-drink combos. Some vending machine providers choose to purchase different types of machines for one location or have one type of machine in multiple locations.

Whatever you decide, it's a good idea for new vending operators to start with a specialty — be it healthy snacks, beverages, or even fresh food — until you learn more about the industry.

To get the most sales, target your offerings to a specific, location-based market. For example, you could stock your food and drink machine at a gym with protein bars and shakes, or stock a vending machine at school with juice and granola bars. You might think of soda and chips when you think of vending machines, but there's money to be made by offering equally convenient, healthy alternatives that people want -- and pay for.

bulk sale

Starting a vending business with machines containing gumballs, stickers, or gumballs - also known as bulk vending - requires very little capital and low maintenance costs.

These usually low-maintenance vending machines might not be glamorous, but the quarters add up. A refurbished vending machine can cost you less than $50 and make up to $30 a month. The products you offer have incredibly low overheads. In the right market - like a school or an amusement park - this modest investment offers the potential for a reliable, passive income stream.

Most bulk vending machines are mechanical devices and require no electricity or battery power to operate, meaning running costs are low to non-existent. However, many candy and toy machines are older, so a used machine may need minor repairs before it is functional.

special sale

You're not just limited to food and beverages when you start a vending business. Large public places like arenas, airports, and shopping malls often have vending machines that offer goods such as tech accessories, beauty products, or other specialty items. Some of these vending machines use the same technology as standard vending machines and some differ from automated vending machines.

Some special sale items include:

Hot Beverages: The sale of coffee or hot beverages is usually most successful in offices, but universities and conference centers are also good locations for this type of vending business. Manufacturers often produce both specialty beverage machines and traditional machines, so you may be able to combine your purchases.

Retail: Essential travel items like phone chargers, headphones, and neck pillows can be lucrative sales items if you can negotiate a deal with a local transit station or even an airport. High-end vending machines in malls and airports often contain luxury skin care products or electronics.

Laundry Detergent: Individually packaged laundry detergent, fabric softener, and dryer sheets sell great when you find the right market for them — like laundromats, condos, or dorms.

Tobacco: Tobacco sales are legal in many states and can be lucrative depending on state taxes. Even cannabis vending machines are also becoming available, but with a much more limited market.

Franchising Options

If you don't want to start your business from scratch, consider purchasing a franchise to start your vending business. As a franchisee, you can work within a proven business framework and receive additional support and training to build your vending business. You can also decide how many or how few machines you want to invest in. However, remember that as a franchisee, you are responsible for paying a portion of your profits to the franchisor.

2. Find the right location for your machine

The type of vending machine you choose is crucial, but where you decide to place that machine is the single most important factor in making a profit from your slots business. For example, an upscale food and beverage machine might fail in a mall full of restaurants, but the same machine might thrive in an office park.

If you're opening a vending machine business, think about the places you've personally purchased something from a vending machine, as well as the times when people are most likely to purchase a drink, snack, or other item. There's a good chance your restaurant choices were limited, you were in a hurry, or you were waiting in a place like the airport or DMV.

Some other location ideas for your vending machine include:

schools

hospitals or medical centers

Supermarket

airports and shopping malls

laundromats

residential complexes

production facilities

The next step is securing the site. A good seller can feel comfortable calling unannounced or inquiring in person about a property or business owner. This approach can work for smaller sites, especially if you're a frequent customer or already know the owner.

You can also try visiting your local Chamber of Commerce. They can give you information about large companies in your area that might give you ideas for potential locations. Ideally, try to place your machine in shops with at least 100 employees or a lot of walk-in customers, e.g. B. in an office park with several companies.

If you already have locations in mind, contact the owners or work to get contact information for the appropriate manager. Discussing location requirements with potential partners can help you better understand local demand and inform your vending and product choices.

Different rules apply to different types of vending machines, and vending regulations vary by state. Before you open a vending machine business and approach potential website owners, find out how your state regulates vendors by contacting your local chamber of commerce or by searching online for your state's small business regulations.

Also, any vending machine you place in a public place may be subject to certain ADA compliance standards, and it's a good idea to keep accessibility in mind when considering vending machine options.

Know the commission requirements and prepare an owner contract

Before you can reap the profits from your vending machine, you must pay a commission to the owner who provides the location and power to run your machine. Typically, you pay the property owner 10% to 25% of the proceeds from your machine.

Whether you want to form an exclusive partnership with a website or not, enter into a contract with the owner that details your agreed upon commission rate, contract length, and the terms you have with the owner.

Also include provisions for breach of contract. It's also wise to include expectations and obligations related to the maintenance and replenishment of your vending machines, vandalism or theft, and the possibility of unprofitability. As always, have a lawyer review the contract before signing it.

3. Find your vending machine

You cannot start a vending machine business without first buying a vending machine. Luckily, finding your vending machine can be as easy as an online search. To get an idea of the different slot offerings and price points, look at both local and national providers. You should also consider inventory costs when looking at vending machine prices.

To find the vending machine of your dreams, start your search with these three types of vendors:

Vending machine manufacturers or wholesalers have the largest selection of vending machines, the latest technology and the most comprehensive supply, repair and training services. However, this is the most expensive option - equipment through vending franchises may require a minimum order of multiple machines or other fees for machine maintenance and entrepreneurial development programs.

Aftermarket sellers or specialist online retailers allow you to browse different makes and models of vending machines and often have helpful resources for business owners.

Consumer-to-consumer platforms like Craigslist and eBay have thousands of vending machines for sale. Save time by filtering by retailer or owner location so you don't have to worry about high shipping costs. This may be the best option for new vending machine users who don't want to spend thousands on a new or refurbished machine.

As you'll quickly discover as you begin your search, vending machines come with a range of features and capabilities, all of which come at different prices.

Some of these features are:

Snack/drink combination machines

Credit card and large billing functionality

Touch or voice access

Remote monitoring software and low stock alerts

Branded "wraps" for the front of your machine

Interactive screens

Don't be too tempted by these special features though, as they can get expensive. Choose the vending machine that best suits the products you want to offer and what you can afford at the moment.

4. Stock your vending machine with inventory

Once you land on a vending machine, you're well on your way to starting a vending business. Next you need to fill it with inventory.

Product selection is a great opportunity to increase sales. Instead of deciding to stock items based on broader food and beverage trends, pay attention to local, location-specific needs. To stay on the safe side, don't overorder stock early and match your supply to demand.

If you choose to offer food and drink combos in your vending machine store, drinks make up the bulk of your sales. As the growing refreshment market expands from soda to coffee, flavored water, and healthier beverages like coconut water, it's worth considering what your location can offer in terms of more expensive specialty drinks and beverages.

Beverage size and shapes affect your machine choices. So if you put a lot of emphasis on selling boxes or irregularly shaped products, try to find a machine with adjustable product size.

5. Explore your financing options

Starting a vending machine business doesn't require nearly as much seed capital as most other small businesses — some businesses can cost hundreds of thousands of dollars to start.

Still, a few thousand dollars isn't exactly small change. If you need credit to purchase your vending machine, consider these two options:

Short-term loan

If you're already a business owner and have your business' financial history to back you up, securing a short-term loan to fund your vending machine may be the best course of action.

Like traditional term loans, short-term lenders deposit a lump sum directly into your commercial bank account, and you pay back your loan plus interest over a set period of time. As you can guess from their name, short-term loans have significantly shorter repayment periods than their long-term counterparts - typically 18 months or less. And the interest rates are slightly higher than on longer-term loans. However, for these reasons, short-term loans are generally easier to qualify than long-term loans.

However, this is a small business loan, so short-term lenders must review and approve your company's finances before agreeing to provide you with a loan. If possible, you should have good business history and good personal credit to prove your candidacy.

equipment financing

You don't necessarily need tons of capital to start a money-making slots business. But if you need a little help, you can apply for an appliance financing loan. The terms of these loans depend on the value of your equipment, which also serves as security in case you default on your loan payments.

With proper care, vending machines can last up to 10 years, which can help lenders insure themselves. If you decide to apply for an equipment loan, you will need quotes for the equipment of the machine(s) you intend to purchase, in addition to your own financial information and business plan. Additionally, if you need capital to purchase inventory, consider inventory financing.

6. Make the right investments

After choosing a location, purchasing a machine, and meeting the placement requirements, you're ready to start a vending machine business - now it's time to focus on making the business profitable.

Invest in a Vending Management System (VMS)

Depending on the technology in your machine, your vending machines may come pre-programmed with management software that allows you to streamline operations, take inventory and track sales.

However, most standard machines require you to manually manage your inventory, which might be doable if you only have a few vending machines. However, once you have five to ten separate vending machines, it's probably a good idea to invest in a vending management system that will help you keep track of your inventory remotely. VMS software allows you to remotely manage your vending machines from any web-enabled device. Most VMS systems provide real-time inventory updates and reporting tools.

Invest in customer service

Even if you only have a vending machine or two, it pays to prioritize customer service with this (or any other) company from the start. To ensure your vending machine is optimized for your customers, all you have to do is follow a few best practices.

Like many location-based businesses, vending machines often rely on word of mouth and personal connections.

Connect with business owners, find your state's sales association, or join local networking groups.

Most importantly, make sure your vending machines are stocked and working weekly or bi-weekly. You might also consider providing an 800 number for service requests and comments, which is a great way to get useful feedback.

Invest your time

Like any other endeavor, starting a vending business requires more than just a capital investment - you must also invest at least some of your time and attention in your vending business.

A full-size vending machine may require you to collect money weekly, which is important when determining how much time you can realistically devote to traveling to places. In addition to the time required to purchase inventory, visit locations, and replenish inventory, running a vending machine business requires you to spend time researching trends in sales, new products, or locations, and collaborating with colleagues.

The typical service cycle for bulk sales—think nonperishable candy or stickers—is anywhere from four to eight weeks. So if you can't break away from your full-time commitments often, bulk selling could be a great way for you to get into the selling business without sacrificing too much time.

Chapter 2

Pros and cons of starting a vending machine business.

With just a few thousand dollars to invest, a vehicle, and determination, you are absolutely capable of starting a vending machine business and making a profit. But starting a slots business isn't all fun and games (although you can sell fun and games in your slot). As with any new venture, there are pros and cons to consider.

Advantages

Easy to Scale: Scaling your slots business is incredibly easy. You can start with a few vending machines and expand the locations as you become more successful.

Variety of choices: Nowadays there are all kinds of slot machines. Vending machines now serve healthy food, gourmet options, and sometimes non-food options as well.

Little to No Overhead: There is little to no overhead to running a vending machine business, especially if you run the business on your own. Because sales businesses don't require many employees or office space, you don't have to worry about payroll, benefits, or rent costs.

Disadvantages

Time Commitment: Running a vending machine business requires that you regularly devote some time and energy to storing, maintaining, and raising funds for your machines.

Theft and Vandalism: Vending machines are easy targets for theft and vandalism. Make sure your machine locations are in safe areas to avoid losing profits.

Chapter 3

frequently asked Questions

1. Are vending machines profitable?

Yes, vending machines can be profitable. The average vending machine makes $35 a week, but vending machines that are well stocked and located in safe, high-traffic locations can bring in over $400 a month.

2. Vending machine owners pay rent?

Yes, vending machine owners pay rent or commission to the building owner.

Machine owners typically pay between 5% and 20% of their machine sales.

3. Are vending machines taxed?

Yes, vending machines are subject to sales tax on the revenue they generate. The amount of sales tax varies by state.

4. Where can you place vending machines?

You can place vending machines in most commercial spaces such as offices, retail stores, bowling alleys and more. But you must first sign a contract with the property owner.

Chapter 4

Advantages of a vending machine shop

Owning anything from a few to a few hundred vending machines can be a manageable, successful business for owners of all skill levels.

The cost of running a vending machine is basically just the cost of the machines and their storage - you don't need office space to house them. Moreover, all you have to do is maintain the machines through repairs, replenish them and collect the money from the transactions.

Before you start: Choose your company structure

When starting a vending machine business, a few machines are the number one purchase. In order to grow your business and legally earn profits and deduct business expenses for tax purposes.